Raising The Bar: The Alma Richards Story

A Journey of Strength, Character, and Relentless Ambition

Frank H. Choi

Copyright Page

All rights reserved. No part of this publication may be reproduced, distributed, or transmitted in any form or by any means, including photocopying, recording, or other electronic or mechanical methods, without the prior written permission of the author, except in the case of brief quotations embodied in critical reviews and certain other noncommercial uses permitted by copyright law.

Copyright © frank H. Choi 2025

Gratitude page

My sincere appreciation extends to all who contributed to this endeavor, both in the making of this book and in the unfolding narrative of Alma Richards' life. His tale is a testament to perseverance, fortitude, and inspiration, and it is a privilege to share it with you.

To Alma's family, for safeguarding his memory and sharing his experiences; to the filmmakers and historians who were instrumental in bringing his story to renewed prominence; and to the numerous individuals whose efforts and commitment have made this book a reality—thank you for your unwavering support.

This book is dedicated to anyone who has confronted hardship, held fast to a grander vision, and strived relentlessly for excellence. Thank you for investing your time in reading this account and for allowing Alma Richards' remarkable journey to ignite your own aspirations.

Disclaimer page

This book is a work of non-fiction based on historical events. While every effort has been made to ensure the accuracy of the information presented, some names, dialogue, and scenes have been dramatized for narrative purposes. All events and characters depicted are based on real-life occurrences, but certain aspects have been reimagined to enhance the storytelling experience.

The author and publisher are not responsible for any errors or omissions that may have occurred during the writing process. Any resemblance to actual persons, living or dead, is purely coincidental, except for historical figures whose actions and accounts are part of the public record.

This book is intended to inform, inspire, entertain, and should not be construed as a definitive historical account.

Table of content

Copyright Page   2

Gratitude page   3

Disclaimer page   4

Introduction   7
   Alma Richards: A Tradition of Resilience and Success   7

Chapter one   12
   Dust of the Valley   12

Chapter two   19
   The Unexpected Spark   19

Chapter three   27
   From Novice to Hopeful   27

Chapter four   34
   Rising Through the Ranks   34

Chapter five   41
   The Games of 1912   41

Chapter six   48
    More Than Just a Jump   48
Chapter seven   55
    The Pull of Academia   55

Chapter eight   63
    Shaping Young Minds   63

Chapter nine   71
    The Genesis of the Film   71

Chapter ten   79
    Lights, Camera, Action   79

Chapter eleven   87
    Echoes of a Remarkable Life   87

Introduction

Alma Richards: A Tradition of Resilience and Success

A little boy named Alma Richards would climb from modest beginnings to make his name known throughout history in the sleepy village of Parowan, Utah, where the untamed landscape meets the expansive heavens. A boy with little potential for greatness by the norms of his era. A student who dropped out of eighth grade to work as a ranch hand in the harsh Utah backcountry. Alma, however, was meant for something much bigger, something the world could not yet comprehend.

Alma's path to Olympic glory started outside, working hard in barns and fields rather than on the gleaming floors of a university. At the start, he wasn't a born athlete. He was not surrounded by possibilities that others would take for granted, nor was he born into riches or luxury. But beyond that seemingly normal demeanor, Alma had something exceptional inside of him—an unwavering will and an unbreakable soul that wouldn't accept anything less than his best.

In addition to being a legendary athlete, Alma Richards became the first person from Utah to win an Olympic gold medal in 1912 at the age of 22. Furthermore, he didn't win it by accident. In the high jump, where the best athletes in the world were supposed to rule, he succeeded. It was truly miraculous that Alma won. With a heart full of desire and little formal training, he traveled to Stockholm. His accomplishment served as evidence of what can occur when the proper time and enthusiasm come together.

However, Alma's tale went beyond the gold medal. It focused on the obstacles he surmounted, both real and imagined. Alma's journey from an uneducated youngster to an Olympic winner embodied the strength of perseverance and overcoming all obstacles. He was able to accomplish the seemingly impossible because of his tenacity and refusal to give up.

More than just athletic ability is symbolized by the picture of Alma jumping into history while wearing the Olympic gold medal around his neck. Anyone who has ever felt like they don't belong, been told they're not good enough or encountered an obstacle that looked insurmountable can find hope in it.

Alma's triumph teaches us that how you play the hand, not the cards you are dealt determines your level of greatness.

We can all relate to Alma's story because of its depth of feeling. His journey from anonymity to international fame is one of perseverance, selflessness, and unshakable dedication. Beyond the records and honors, however, Alma's narrative is one of a man who forged his route by defying expectations and demonstrating that the seemingly impossible is achievable, rather than by taking the well-traveled path of his contemporaries.

Alma Richards personified the energy of a whole age as the globe witnessed him soar into the skies during the Olympics in 1912. a mindset that prioritized emulating the virtues of diligence, humility, and tenacity over merely taking home gold. Alma had no intention of becoming famous. He wasn't looking for attention. All he wanted was to show himself and everyone around him that he was more capable than they had ever thought.

In addition to exploring Alma Richards' incredible athletic accomplishments, this book provides a compelling portrayal of a man who was equally as concerned with his heart as his physical prowess.

Alma was loyal to himself through all of the highs and lows, and generations after his death are still motivated by his genuineness. From his Olympic achievements to his strong commitment to his family, Alma's life was one of conviction, determination, and an unyielding trust in his potential.

Every dreamer, every underdog, and everyone who has ever encountered a challenge too great to conquer can learn from Alma Richards' story. It teaches us that what matters is how far you're willing to go to realize your aspirations, not where you're from or what you lack. Alma left behind an enduring legacy, and his life—both on and off the track—is proof of the ability of one person to overcome hardship and motivate others.

We are reminded that the journey is just as significant as the destination as we reflect on Alma Richards' life and the significant influence he had on the sports industry and beyond. From the fields of Parowan, Utah, to the Olympic podium in Stockholm, Alma's adventure changed his life forever and served as an inspiration to countless sportsmen and dreamers.

This book is a celebration of the principles that shaped Alma—the tenacity, the fervor, and the calm strength that characterized him—rather than merely recounting his achievements. His achievement was not achieved suddenly; rather, it was the result of years of perseverance, selflessness, and faith in his skills. Alma Richards demonstrated that anything is achievable with enough will and passion.

And as you read this tale, may it encourage you to aim higher, run faster like Alma, never settle for anything less than excellence.

Chapter one

Dust of the Valley

The Parowan Soil: Life and Scenery in Utah at the Turn of the Century

Parowan, Utah, seemed to be stuck in a bygone era, tucked away between the vast desert and the tall mountains. Families were bonded by the land they worked and the principles they upheld in the small town at the turn of the century, which exuded a spirit of tough self-reliance. The harsh sun above, the wind in the air, and the soil beneath their feet determined not only how they lived their everyday lives but also how they survived. Their identity was molded by the environment, which created a manner of life that was both harsh and exquisite.

The town of Parowan was not for the weak of heart. Under the shadow of the towering Pine Valley Mountains, Southern Utah's undulating hills were peppered with pine trees and the occasional herd of cattle. For those who lived there, the soil, which was full of red dust and dirt, was essential to life.

Despite its harshness, the country was home. Families worked in the fields, producing what they could in a harsh environment. The sweat and hardship of daily labor held the close-knit group together.

This environment was a frequent companion and a challenge to Alma Wilford Richards. The hard realities and serene beauty of the area influenced his formative years. His early years were filled with the repetitive hum of the plow breaking the dirt, the sounds of cattle blowing, and the wind rustling through the sagebrush. Alma had an innate bond with Parowan's soil that went beyond just geography. His family had to make ends meet, much like a lot of other families in the region. They put a lot of effort into taming the ground and bringing life to what frequently appeared to be more dust than soil.

Despite its dryness and cracks, the Parowan soil was alive. Families, animals, and harvests all benefited from it. However, it also came at a high cost to those who worked it. Adversity was nothing new to the people of Parowan. To put food on the table, they battled the dust, the heat, and the sun every day. However, Alma would discover a greater sense of purpose in this very fight.

Alma's destiny was shaped by more than just the land. The boy's development was greatly influenced by his family, the principles they upheld, and the church they attended. He inherited a strong work ethic and a sense of independence from his parents. They instilled in him the principles that would guide him throughout his life: the significance of community, family, and faith.

Alma was always being pulled onward by something greater, even though life in Parowan was simple and harsh. It was the first hints of ambition, the subdued murmurs of something greater, something outside the valley's bounds. It was his conviction that he could transcend the arduous labor and dusty fields that characterized so many people's lives in Parowan.

Young Alma: Farm Days and the Beginnings of Ambition

Alma Richards was not fortunate or comfortable from birth. He spent his early years working hard with his family, doing seemingly never-ending chores, much like a lot of other boys his age. The labor that life required was nothing new to him. The young child labored in the fields from dawn to dusk, repairing fences, caring for animals, and delivering water to the crops. There was little time for frivolity in a life that demanded every last bit of energy. However, there was a subdued sense of pride in Alma's work, a sense of fulfillment in knowing that he was making a significant contribution and that his family depended on him.

However, Alma was unique even as a little child. While others were content with their lives, Alma's thoughts frequently strayed outside the valley's boundaries. After a hard day, he would lie in the hayloft and look out at the far-off hills, wondering what was out there. Alma had a dream about a universe that was larger than his own. Like the crops he assisted in growing on the farm, his dreams started to grow in the rich soil of his thoughts.

Alma's need for something more was stoked by the small things, those brief periods of introspection. However, a fortuitous meeting would permanently alter his life. Arriving in Parowan on a seemingly routine journey was a visiting professor from Michigan. However, for Alma, the encounter ignited a fire within him that would burn brightly for the rest of his life.

Alma's work ethic and innate athleticism pleased the professor, who recognized something in the boy that others would have missed. He urged Alma to think more deeply about his schooling and to look beyond the fields and farms that had previously characterized his life. Despite its seeming simplicity, this encounter sowed the seeds of Alma's desire.

Attending school, let alone doing well in it, seemed like an unattainable ideal for a boy who had never received much formal schooling. But that day, something inside Alma clicked. He became aware that he had other options outside the one he was on. He was determined to find a method to get to the world of potential that lay beyond the valley. With the support of the professor and his aspirations for more, Alma's ambition started to blossom.

Even though Alma had dropped out of school early to support his family, the notion of going back to school became popular. The idea of competing in the world outside of Parowan had evolved from a fantasy to a real objective that he could work toward. Alma's life was going to change due to the desire to succeed that suddenly burned within him, not only his strong work ethic or his family's encouragement.

His ambition started to take shape as he grew older. He looked for fresh chances and seized every opportunity to develop and learn. After receiving a scholarship at Cornell University, he would immerse himself in intellectual endeavors and work toward a law degree. Alma, however, never lost sight of the values he learned on the Parowan farm—the value of perseverance, hard effort, and self-belief—despite his academic achievements.

Alma will soon be poised on the edge of something even bigger in the Cornell hallways. He was more than simply a boy from a tiny town because of his time on the farm and the hours he spent cultivating the soil. It had made him into an athlete, a person with the fortitude, tenacity, and will to go beyond the confines of his childhood. He would go farther than the land could, nevertheless, because of his inner strength.

Alma Richards will achieve grandeur from the very dust of the valley, from the modest life of a small child with lofty dreams. It was not always obvious where his journey would take him, and it was not an easy one. However, Alma's tale, which is one of tenacity, drive, and conviction that anything is possible, serves as a powerful reminder to all of us of the value of pursuing our goals regardless of our background.

Chapter two

The Unexpected Spark

A Ranch Hand's Diversion from Destiny: Getting Off the Plow

Alma Richards had always understood the value of diligence. Like the red dirt under his boots, he was accustomed to the sound of the ancient wooden plow groaning, the constant beat of the horses' hooves, and the rough, worn handle of the rake. The seasons defined life in Parowan, Utah, where I grew up. Planting, caring for, and harvesting produced a cycle that required daily attention and work. This cycle—the quiet, hard work that nourished his family and met their most basic needs—was the focus of Alma's early years. When your hands were always coated in mud, there wasn't much space for distractions or dreams.

Nevertheless, Alma couldn't get rid of the sense that there was more to life than this, despite all the labor and sweat that came with being a farmer. It wasn't that he didn't like his job or thought it was unimportant; rather, the farm had given him a sense of direction and the land had influenced many aspects of his personality. But the issue was that, like his body, Alma's intellect had become restless. The fire that slowly started to develop within him was too strong for the dust of Parowan, despite it having been a constant companion to his youth.

He had to drop out of school early because his family needed him. However, Alma now yearned for something different because this decision was really necessary. A silent longing was starting to tug at him, but he didn't want to leave his family. Something had ignited a dream within him, a glimmering ember on the horizon. It wasn't about running away from his obligations; rather, it was about looking for something that was outside the parameters of the life he was familiar with, an opportunity to develop outside of the farm, and the straightforward, industrious life that had always been the foundation of his existence. Now, the question was, where was he going? How could he?

Leaving the plow behind felt unthinkable at first. The farm served as his foundation, and the land was all he knew. Even if his existence was based on hard effort, Alma couldn't shake the nagging feeling that it could be better than this. Although he had no idea where this route would take him or what would happen, he felt an irresistible pull—a tug of fate—that caused him to start thinking about other options. It was about accepting a life he hadn't yet dreamed of, not about rejecting the one he already had.

Although Alma was unaware of it at the time, the uneasy sensation that something more was in store for him would eventually result in an unanticipated meeting that would permanently change the trajectory of his life. The unassuming ranch hand would become an athlete and eventually an Olympic champion—it was a flame that, once lit, would burn brilliantly. But he had to take the initial step—moving away from the plow and into the unknown—before he could pursue that ambition.

A Fortuitous Meeting: The Scholar Who Observed More

Alma was walking into town one afternoon to run errands for his family. Even though it was a tiny town and everyone knew one another, it was still uncommon for a young ranch hand like Alma, who didn't have the same formal education as other people in the area, to come into town by himself.

Alma was walking through Parowan's muddy streets when he noticed a man. He was not like the other residents of the town. Certainly a stranger—someone whose attire and demeanor distinguished him from the industrious people of Parowan. Unlike Alma, who wore dirty jeans and boots, this man donned a suit that seemed out of place to the locals.

The professor, as Alma would later call him, was a tourist who was in town on his way to somewhere else. Alma was interested in the man's presence, even if he didn't know who he was at the moment. His name was Professor Hensley. Alma was accustomed to the harsh, everyday realities of Parowan life, where discussions frequently focused on the weather, animals, or agricultural output. However, this individual had a different energy and viewpoint when he spoke. His thoughts appeared to float around the potential of the future, what might be, and what ought to be, rather than the mundane routine of farm life.

As luck would have it, Alma and the professor started talking. At first, it was just a friendly conversation, but Professor Hensley saw something about Alma's manner. This young man, who was a native of the land and had sunburned skin and calloused hands, had a gentle curiosity that spoke of a mind that had not yet been fully awakened, yet there was also intensity in his gaze. This young ranch worker seemed to be pining for something more than the plow, and the professor, who was academic, couldn't help but notice it.

"Young man, what do you dream of?" Professor Hensley inquired in a contemplative tone.

The question caused Alma's forehead to wrinkle. Have a dream? What could one dream about? For the most part, he had embraced the life that had been delivered to him—the farm. His family relied on him because he worked the farm. However, something was suddenly stirring deep within him. Uncertain of what to say, he paused before responding.

Alma answered somewhat sheepishly, "I've never really thought about it." "All I do is work the land." That's what we do.

The professor looked at Alma, his eyes growing deeper as he nodded. "The land is significant. I don't dispute that. However, life is much more than the ground beneath your feet, and the globe is huge. There are concepts, opportunities, and futures out there just waiting for you to explore. Your origins don't have to determine who you are.

Alma felt a flame ignite within him as the words lingered in the air. It had been offered for the first time that his life might be more. That the plow and the land weren't the only things that defined him. His imagination started to form the notion of something bigger, of a world outside Parowan's borders.

Professor Hensley was not a man who spoke inanely. He spoke honestly because he thought Alma had potential and that there was more to him than the outside world had yet to discover. He talked about education and the possibilities that come with persistence and knowledge. Alma's ability to do more than work the fields was initially indicated by the lecturer. He could study, learn, and succeed in ways he never would have imagined.

The lecturer remarked, "I think you could be something extraordinary, Alma," as though addressing a fellow scholar. "You possess the motivation and the spirit. Right now, you need guidance.

Alma kept thinking about the terms "extraordinary," "spirit," and "drive" long after the professor had left town. Alma had been profoundly affected by the seemingly insignificant experience. It had given him a burning drive to overcome his situation. He started to imagine a future outside of the Parowan fields for the first time. He started to perceive himself as someone capable of more than just being a laborer or a ranch hand.

Alma came to the realization that his life wasn't predestined during that brief encounter. He had to decide whether to continue along the same path he had always known or to take a different one where his destiny could be shaped by ambition, willpower, and knowledge. His trip would no longer be limited to the confines of the farm after the spark was ignited.

Alma had become more aware of something after hearing Professor Hensley's remarks. They had sown a seed that would sprout and lead him to success in the future. The aspirations he had previously suppressed, concealed behind the burden of accountability, now gained new vitality. Alma was now a young man with the potential to become a star, not just a ranch hand who tilled the land. The lecturer had demonstrated to him that he

25

might strive for his fate rather than it being predetermined. Alma would also never turn around.

The path to greatness had started with a straightforward chat—a conversation that ignited the unanticipated spark that would ultimately transform Alma's life forever—rather than with extravagant gestures or promises of success.

Chapter three

From Novice to Hopeful

Finding a Natural Talent on the Field with First Jumps

Alma Richards was a resilient person. His strength was derived from the land itself, not from lifting weights or working out throughout the day. It was the strength that came from working long hours under the merciless sun, breaking the ground with a plow, subduing obstinate livestock, and transporting water to dry crops. The muscles in his back and the calluses on his hands weren't acquired the conventional way, but they were just as genuine. And Alma's path to greatness would be greatly influenced by her quiet, underlying strength.

Alma never considered himself an athlete, at least not in the conventional sense, despite his diligence and physical prowess. He measured the seasons by the crops he planted, collected, and stored; the farm was his life. The world he knew had no place for competition or sports. He was more passionate about his work than he was about the games and exercises that other people found fascinating. But when he leaped—not just a literal one, but a leap of faith into the uncharted territory of athletics—everything changed.

There was no pomp or dramatic event when Alma's gift was discovered. It was more of a quiet moment that had been building for years than a planned occasion. As is often the case with outstanding players who appear out of thin air, it happened on the sports field. Alma was fascinated but unclear about what he was meant to do when he found himself standing at the edge of a high jump one day. He had not received high jump training; instead, he had jumped more naturally and out of need. However, something clicked when he threw himself over the bar.

Alma didn't have high hopes for the jump. It was merely a haphazard attempt at something so alien to him. He lacked the luxury of formal instruction and was not a skilled athlete. Even he was taken aback by the ease and effortless grace with which he moved once his feet were off the ground. He easily cleared the bar as he soared higher than he had anticipated. Although by no means flawless, it was indisputable. Alma had briefly tapped into something special, something that was outside the scope of his regular employment.

The sensation was strong and instantaneous. Alma felt what could only be called a sensation of liberation during that fleeting instant of time when he was suspended in midair. It was the result of years of arduous labor, the accumulation of strength and energy, and something that was hidden deep inside him—a natural talent that had been waiting to be found. He hadn't even given the high jump any thought, let alone been aiming for it. But in that moment, he realized that he had discovered a gift that would forever alter his life—something he had never realized he possessed.

At that point, Alma started to consider himself an athlete as well as a farm lad. It was not an abrupt change, nor did the realization occur suddenly. It was a calm daybreak instead. Alma was aware of his physical prowess, but he had discovered something more: the capacity to soar, to transcend, to be more than a mere laborer. The leap was more than just a flight of fancy; it was a leap into a new phase of his life, one that was full of opportunity and promise.

Early Training: Developing Power and an Unusual Approach

Following that initial leap, Alma's life started to change in small but significant ways. He was enraged by the unadulterated brilliance he saw on the field. Knowing that he had talent was insufficient; he wanted to comprehend it, develop it, and realize its full potential. Alma's journey, however, was anything from conventional. There were no pricey training regimens or flashy coaches. Rather, Alma started her training in the most fundamental and useful way possible: by putting in more effort.

Alma wasn't quite sure where to start at first. He didn't receive any official training for the high jump or any other sport, for that matter. He had not been exposed to the types of methods or approaches that others could have picked up at gyms or schools. He knew very little and had very little experience. Alma, however, was unfazed. He made up for his lack of academic knowledge with perseverance and a desire to learn. He trained the same way he always had: by working hard and pushing himself past his comfort zone.

Alma's initial training phase focused on building his body to satisfy the high jump's requirements. He already had a foundation of strength and endurance from his work as a ranch hand, but the high jump demanded a new type of power—explosive energy that would lift him over the bar and skyward. Alma started concentrating on strengthening his legs, putting forth endless effort to develop the muscles that would enable him to soar higher. His leaps became more forceful as his legs got stronger. However, the jump itself required skill, which Alma had to acquire by trial and error; it wasn't just about physical might.

Alma's training was a little out of the ordinary because she didn't have a coach. He experimented with several methods and gradually improved them, relying largely on his intuition. Alma had to learn on his own, creating a style that was all his own, unlike other sportsmen who might have had access to official instruction. He didn't employ the techniques taught in textbooks by professional players. Rather, Alma's approach was unvarnished, organic, and brimming with vitality derived from his strong bond with the land and the physical labor that had molded him.

Alma's ability to blend strength and quickness was one of the training's most obvious features. He was flexible due to his muscular upbringing on the farm, which enabled him to alter conventional high jump methods to fit his own body. He used the momentum of his own body to propel himself higher, relying not only on the strength of his legs but also on his ability to precisely sequence his movements. Although it was an unconventional strategy, it was successful. Alma's skill was evident, and he was reaching heights that many others found difficult.

His training was a never-ending cycle of experimentation and development. On the field, he would rehearse by jumping over improvised bars that he had constructed himself. He was constantly pushing himself and trying to get better. He would get a bit better, a little stronger, and a little higher every day. His development of mental toughness, however, was arguably the most beneficial aspect of his training. He was educating his mind to think that he could accomplish something amazing in addition to exercising his body. His success was largely due to such belief. Alma's idea that he might reach greatness drove all of his efforts, and he wasn't merely hoping for a decent jump.

Alma's trip reflected his character in many ways. Alma viewed his lack of formal training as a challenge rather than a barrier, as others would have thought. His confidence increased with each successful leap as he accepted the process and enjoyed the task itself. There were moments when it was difficult to improve his technique. There were setbacks, and periods of uncertainty when the jump seemed too challenging or the bar too high. Alma, however, never faltered in her resolve. He was just trying to be better than he had been the day before, not aiming to be flawless.

His training was anything but traditional, but it was precisely this unconventional method that helped him develop into the athlete he would become. He always set out to forge his path rather than take the conventional one. Alma Richards had taken the first significant steps toward something spectacular, going from a novice with no formal instruction to a hopeful challenger with the potential to become great.

Chapter four

Rising Through the Ranks

Beyond Brigham Young: Perfecting the Art

Alma Richards did not achieve brilliance in a straight line. It was about grit, self-discovery, and the unwavering quest for something more than oneself. Following his first attempt at high jumping, Alma realized that skill by itself wouldn't get him where he wanted to go. Even if the Parowan fields had equipped him with the physical prowess and determination to face obstacles, his future would be shaped by his education, discipline, and development of his innate talents.

He had shown potential already. His power and high jumps were indisputable, but now he needed to take those foundational skills and hone them into a skill that would enable him to compete internationally. Alma's undeveloped talent was refined into the disciplined form of a world-class athlete during his time at Brigham Young University (BYU). Alma started honing his abilities here.

Alma started a new chapter in his life at Brigham Young, where formal education and training were now direct realities rather than simply ideas. His mind could now finally match his goal because he was enrolled in a demanding academic environment. However, the hours he spent honing his athletic skills were equally as significant as his academic pursuits. Alma first experienced the coaching and mentoring that would help him transform from a gifted athlete to a polished one at BYU.

The BYU coaching was absolutely revolutionary. Alma had demonstrated his capacity to leap high, but he now needed instruction on how to channel his energy and manage the explosive power that came naturally to him. The high jump required timing, skill, and accuracy in addition to strength. Alma didn't have these abilities at first, but he started to acquire them with the correct guidance.

coaches helped him analyze every facet of the high jump since they saw his potential. To turn his innate athleticism into something more dependable and efficient, they taught him how to approach the bar, refine his form, and precisely time his takeoff. His movements had changed from being impulsive and frantic to deliberate and planned. Alma gained knowledge of the art of high jumping, and each practice gave him fresh approaches to enhance his performance.

Alma discovered the value of mental discipline in addition to the jump's mechanics. He learned how to approach each leap with a concentrated, unwavering perspective from the training he got at BYU, in addition to how to jump higher. His academic and athletic preparation combined with the mental toughness he had acquired from his years on the farm when every day was an endurance challenge, created a well-rounded person. Alma was developing into an athlete in the traditional meaning of the word, not merely a ranch worker who had discovered a knack.

It wasn't an easy transition from country boy to collegiate athlete. Alma encountered challenges that put his emotional and mental fortitude to the test in addition to his physical limitations. He had to strike a balance between the demands of exercise and academics, and occasionally his body hurt, his mind became tired, and doubt began to creep in. However, Alma's inner strength—cultivated over years of arduous work and perseverance—came to the fore at these times. He persevered in the face of hardship because he knew that if he kept going, he would eventually achieve his goals.

Alma's undeveloped talent was transformed into something spectacular during his time at Brigham Young University. It served as the cornerstone for his subsequent achievements. BYU gave him the setting he needed to hone his skills, strengthen his mental fortitude, and acquire the self-discipline needed for the international arena. The drive to Stockholm was the next step he was prepared to take.

The Path to Stockholm: Getting Ready for the Global Arena

By the time Alma Richards finished his collegiate training at BYU, he had developed into a formidable athlete. His high-jumping achievements had started to attract notice. Years of coaching and self-motivation had honed his natural talent, making him a formidable competitor. But he needed more than local notoriety to reach his ultimate goal—to compete in the Olympics. He had to establish himself on the international scene.

37

Alma had his sights set on competing in the running high jump event at the 1912 Olympics in Stockholm, which were drawing near. It would not be simple. Many of the competitors Alma would compete against had years of formal training, better facilities, and more money, so the competition was intense. However, Alma possessed a quality that none of them could readily imitate: his unwavering work ethic and the mental toughness to get past any challenge that stood in his way.

Instead of being characterized by spectacular events, the road to Olympic qualification was a succession of challenges that put Alma's skills, determination, and faith in his abilities to the test. Alma had to compete against the top athletes from throughout the United States in national events to qualify. Alma's skills would be put to the test in these competitions.

Alma would compete against some of the best high jumpers in the nation at the U.S. Olympic Trials, the first of these events. Alma was prepared despite the tremendous strain. Years of training had brought him to this position, which was the result of his perseverance, dedication, and unwavering ambition.

Alma gave an amazing performance at the trials. He distinguished himself from the other athletes not only by his high jumps but also by his control and consistency. Brigham Young University's years of polishing had paid off. He had perfect form, a deliberate attitude, and a precise technique. Alma's leaps were more than just a display of strength; they were a kind of art, the ideal fusion of might and elegance.

He was able to overcome the pressure because of his resolve, which had been developed over years of arduous struggle. He easily cleared the qualifying height, guaranteeing his spot on the American Olympic squad. It was his fantasy moment, the one that would transport him from the dusty plains of Parowan to the Olympic stage in Stockholm.

Not only was Alma's Olympic qualification a personal success, but it was also a victory for everyone who had ever questioned him and thought of him as merely a small-town ranch worker. His triumph served as a reminder that greatness might come from anywhere and that it was determined more by tenacity and conviction than by status or money. Alma was now ready to compete at the greatest level after rising through the ranks.

Although the path to Stockholm was not a smooth one, Alma's journey was characterized by the challenges and victories he faced along the way. His transition from an aspirational athlete to an Olympic contender began with his qualification for the Games. Alma knew that the real test was coming as he set his sights on the magnificent stage. Alma was prepared to take on the obstacles that awaited him in Stockholm, though, because of the preparation, perseverance, and unshakeable faith that had gotten him this far.

For Alma Richards, the trip to the Olympics was a spiritual one as much as a physical one. He had climbed through the ranks, overcome the odds, and demonstrated to the world that even the most unlikely people can achieve greatness.

Chapter five

The Games of 1912

An International Gathering: The Olympic Ambience in Stockholm

In the summer of 1912, an unusual assembly took place. The Stockholm Olympics welcomed competitors from throughout the world to compete in the center of Sweden. There was a sense of purpose, tension, and excitement in the air. Only resurrected in 1896, the Olympic Games were still relatively young, but by 1912, they were starting to establish themselves as the highest level of athletic competition. The competition brought people from all over the world together to demonstrate human power, speed, and endurance, but it also served as a symbol of solidarity and camaraderie. It was a chance for nations to unite under the common bond of sport and set aside their differences.

The size of the event was amply demonstrated by Stockholm's Olympic Stadium. The stands were packed with thousands of fans, and the noise of their applause could be heard throughout the arena.

Anticipation permeated the air as flags from every country flapped in the breeze. The athletes who had come to compete, however, felt a sense of pressure beneath the majesty of the opening ceremonies and the performances that would follow. They saw the Games as an opportunity to create history rather than merely demonstrate their abilities.

The magnitude of the scenario was not lost on Alma Richards, who stood at the edge of the high jump pit under the shadow of the stadium's imposing structure. He had risen from modest origins in Parowan, Utah when aspirations of international fame appeared far off and unlikely. And now here he was, on the biggest platform of all, one of the world's greatest athletes. For a young man who had grown up working the land and laboring in the fields, it was an unreal experience to be suddenly vying for the greatest sporting accolades. Even though he was surrounded by the greatest in the world and on the edge of glory, his thoughts were only on the task at hand: setting the record straight and earning his place in Olympic history.

As Alma became used to the arena's repetitive noises, the throng was a blur. He mentally prepared for his jumps with razor-sharp intensity. Alma could feel the weight of the moment beneath the electrified atmosphere. The athletes' anxiousness was evident as the stadium throbbed with activity. Alma found it both empowering and humbling to realize that he had earned the opportunity to be on the stage for something big.

The Games were a celebration of the human spirit in Stockholm. For the athletes, it was an opportunity to push themselves to the edge, to see how strong they could be and how strong they could be. This was the result of years of self-belief, sacrifice, and hard work for Alma. He was now a competitor who had earned his spot on the world stage and was determined to take advantage of the chance, not just a ranch hand with a natural knack for jumping.

Contrary to Expectations: The Day Alma Richards Made History

More than just an athletic test, the high jump competition at the 1912 Olympics was a show of willpower and resolve, and it would prove to be the turning point in Alma Richards' career. The athletes he fought were among the best the world had ever seen, and the competition was intense. Alma stood out, though, with a quiet confidence that had been developed over years of hard effort and a belief in his abilities that was difficult to shake. The goal on the day of the tournament was to prove to himself that he belonged, not to prove anyone else wrong.

The world appeared to vanish when Alma took her first steps up to the high jump bar in the Olympic arena. He had participated in tryouts and lesser competitions, but nothing like the Olympics. Despite the tremendous strain, Alma had mastered the art of managing it from his years of training. He shut out the world's distractions, the clamor of the crowd, and the dazzling sunlight above to concentrate on the task at hand. It was his time.

Even the most experienced high jumpers would have found the bar difficult to reach. Alma was prepared to challenge himself further, though, as he had been jumping higher and higher during his training sessions at Brigham Young. He got a running start, his eyes fixed on the bar, and moved with the fluid, trained motion that had become instinctive to him. Alma's torso arched elegantly through the air as his legs gave him a powerful boost.

As Alma flew higher and crossed the bar with an ease that seemed simple, the crowd fell silent. He realized he had cleared the bar as soon as his feet touched the floor. Alma Richards had not only overcome the height but also his doubts with the leap. He had established the tone for one of the most outstanding Olympic performances ever.

However, Alma's manner and technique were what captured the attention of onlookers, not only his jump. Alma's strategy was different from many of the other athletes who followed the conventional high jump techniques. Through a combination of the polished training he had received at Brigham Young and the raw athleticism he had learned on the farm, he had developed an unconventional technique. He stood out from the others due to his natural timing, instinctual manner, and capacity to blend strength with quickness. It became more and more obvious that Alma was a formidable opponent as he continued to reach ever-higher altitudes.

The heights kept getting higher, and Alma had to overcome a new obstacle with every leap. Alma was unfazed by his unrelenting competitors. With every leap, he got one step closer to winning the gold medal and realizing the dream he had been pursuing for years. With every successful jump, his confidence increased, and by the time the bar reached the ultimate height, Alma was certain that he could claim it.

Alma inhaled deeply and readied himself for his last leap, with the bar raised higher than before. As he ran down the runway, his legs pounding with strength, the audience held its breath. The leap that would guarantee his place in Olympic history was this one. As Alma's body twisted and turned in midair, he launched himself into the air. The crowd's clamor was deafening as his feet cleared the bar.

Alma landed gently on the mat, and time seemed to stop instantly. He had succeeded in winning the gold medal in the high jump, making him the first Utahn to win an Olympic gold medal. In addition to making history for himself, Alma Richards had also made history for his state, his nation, and the innumerable athletes who would come after him.

Alma couldn't help but think back on the lengthy journey that had brought him to this point as he stood on the stage with the national anthem playing. Every stride from the Parowan fields to the magnificent stadium in Stockholm had put his fortitude, tenacity, and faith in his abilities to the test. And now that he had the gold medal around his neck, Alma Richards had shown the world that everything was achievable with perseverance, hard effort, and the will to try something new.

In addition to being a personal achievement, Alma's high jump win at the 1912 Olympics served as motivation for future generations of competitors. It was a triumph against all difficulties, demonstrating the strength of tenacity and the spirit of rivalry. Alma Richards had jumped into history and demonstrated to the world what was possible if one dared to dream.

Chapter six

More Than Just a Jump

A Golden Return: Praise and Fresh Possibilities

Before Alma Richards' triumph proved a turning point in his life and the history of American sports, the thunderous cheers of the Stockholm crowd had hardly subsided. It wasn't simply a physical thing that broke when Alma's successful leap caused the high jump bar to finally fall to the ground; it was a barrier that had long stood in his way of receiving the recognition he so richly earned. Alma was more than just an Olympic champion—he was now a legend, a representation of the strength of tenacity and unadulterated ability. His 1912 victory was more than simply a high jump gold medal; it was a victory for anybody who had ever been told that their origins or limitations prevented them from becoming great.

When Olympic champion Alma returned to the United States, he met with the kind of awe that few athletes ever encounter. Newspapers celebrated his win, and almost every sports fan in the country was mentioning him. The modest farm lad from Parowan, Utah, was no longer Alma. He had demonstrated that success could be achieved without the support of a wealthy or illustrious family, and he was now a symbol of pride for the country. Far more valuable were Alma's unwavering attitude and his conviction that he could overcome all obstacles. That belief was confirmed by the gold medal he wore around his neck.

When he returned, Alma's increased notoriety gave him access to prospects he had never thought possible. Alma realized that the life he had known before—the life of a ranch hand, the life of toiling on the farm—would never be the same as he got off the train and entered the embrace of his loved ones. With his victory, a new chapter had begun, one that held difficulties and thrilling opportunities outside of the Olympic podium.

In addition to becoming Alma famous in the sports world, his victory made him a household name who was respected for his narrative and praised for his accomplishments. However, new expectations accompanied that praise. People were curious about the man who had overcome all difficulties and climbed to the top of the Olympic podium from the arid fields of Parowan. Alma became well-known and was invited to social gatherings, meet with politicians, and even take part in open demonstrations of his athletic ability. In addition to winning an Olympic gold medal, Alma was a living example of the American ideal, and his tale spoke to anybody who had ever faced hardship and wished for a brighter future.

Alma, however, had no intention of reveling in his newfound celebrity. It had nothing to do with the attention, the banquets, or the awards. The goal was to keep moving forward. He knew deep down that winning a gold medal wasn't the end of the road. His achievements were but a prelude to the future he saw, one that would require more than mere athletic ability. Alma realized that utilizing the chances given to you to broaden your views and have a significant influence was the key to success in life rather than sitting on your laurels.

In the years after his Olympic victory, Alma rose to prominence in the intellectual and professional spheres in addition to the sporting world. After graduating from Cornell University with a law degree, he went back to school and started teaching at Venice High School in Los Angeles. Those around him had found inspiration in Alma's narrative, and he was resolved to use his position to help others. His work as a teacher, mentor, and public figure would be built upon the principles he had acquired in life and on the track.

The golden return was about the opportunities that came about as a result of Alma's achievement, not just about the recognition or sudden celebrity. He was given the chance to continue the job that had shaped his character long before he won the gold medal and to effect long-lasting change. Alma made use of his position to support others, uplift young athletes, and demonstrate to them that anyone who was prepared to put in the necessary effort could achieve success.

Unleashing Versatility: Examining Different Sports

Alma Richards was never one to sit back and enjoy his success. He could have easily let his gold medal define him for the rest of his life after reaching the height of his achievement in the high jump at the 1912 Olympics. In his field, he had achieved the pinnacle of success. But Alma had never been that kind of man. His story was not merely about one sport; rather, it was about his continuous development and diversification as well as his quest to surpass the boundaries he had already overcome.

His continual pursuit of challenges outside of the high jump demonstrated his versatility as an athlete. Once focused on the discipline of jumping, his natural talent was now being tested in other sports. Alma's accomplishments were not restricted to a single sport; his experience working on farms had given him a strong, adaptable body that enabled him to succeed in a variety of activities. Being good at one thing wasn't enough for him; he was constantly looking for new ways to challenge himself, learn new things, and overcome obstacles.

versatility started to show in the decathlon, a track and field competition that called for a variety of abilities, such as strength, running, throwing, and jumping. Because it required mastery in a variety of disciplines, the decathlon was frequently regarded as the pinnacle of an athlete's total athleticism. This assignment was the ideal chance for Alma to demonstrate his skills and push himself to the maximum.

Alma entered the decathlon with the same humility and commitment that had gotten him through his previous preparation, even if he had achieved success in the high jump. It was more about pushing his limits and seeing how far he could go than it was about competing with others. He was a strong competitor in a number of the decathlon events due to his innate athleticism, but what distinguished him was his mental toughness. Alma did not shy away from hard effort or use shortcuts. Rather, he approached every task with the attitude of someone who had already demonstrated his abilities and was prepared to do it once more, but on a wider scale this time.

Alma's decathlon experience was only one instance of his constant pursuit of new obstacles to overcome. He also experimented with other sports, such as hurdling and running, because he was constantly keen to broaden his skill set and observe how his body would respond to various physical demands. Alma was a true athlete in every way, not just a high jumper, and his openness to trying new things contributed to his reputation as one of the most adaptable and committed athletes of his era.

He never performed as well in the decathlon as he did in the high jump, but his willingness to participate in a variety of sports said a lot about his personality. It was more about demonstrating to himself that he could become proficient in all facets of his athleticism than it was about taking home numerous medals. Alma's adaptability reflected his belief that there is always more space for improvement, regardless of where one begins or the obstacles one encounters. Alma had the option of staying a one-event athlete, but his dedication to developing into a well-rounded competitor made him a more resilient and whole person.

Alma Richards' influence in the years following his Olympic triumph extended much beyond his gold medal. His legacy as an Olympic champion and as a man who led a life characterized by a quest for perfection in everything was solidified by his experimentation with different sports endeavors, his work as a teacher, and his commitment to developing the next generation of athletes. His narrative was about more than simply her high jump; it was about her conviction that, if one was up to the task, greatness could be attained in a variety of ways.

Chapter seven

The Pull of Academia

From the Field to the Classroom: The Search for Information

Alma Richards had a difficult journey from the dusty pastures of Parowan, Utah, to the esteemed halls of Cornell University. Alma's unwavering determination to develop both academically and physically characterized the journey, which was also characterized by sweat, hard effort, and the rare moment of uncertainty. He was already well-known outside of the sports world after winning the gold in the high jump in the 1912 Stockholm Olympics. However, he wasn't genuinely inspired by the recognition and attention. He was motivated to pursue additional schooling by his quiet quest for knowledge and his conviction that he could be more than merely an Olympic athlete.

Alma had already shown that he was a capable athlete. Although he had mastered the high jump and achieved heights that few could match, Alma knew deep down that he had another goal in mind.

He had come from a working-class background where education was considered a luxury. He had dropped out of school early to assist his family in the fields, but Alma had learned over the years that although a man might be sustained by hard work, he could be transformed by knowledge. Being physically strong and capable was insufficient. Alma was aware that he needed to continue to grow intellectually to be fully well-rounded.

The choice was not made right away. For a man who had lived with dirt beneath his fingernails and the burden of hard work on his shoulders for the majority of his life, the academic world appeared far away, even alien. However, a seed had been sown by Alma's interactions with individuals such as Professor Hensley, who had shown him the opportunities outside of the farm. He was motivated to pursue something that had always seemed just out of his grasp by this spark. For him, education had evolved into a new kind of objective that called for a distinct set of abilities, abilities that Alma would eventually learn.

The route to a university was a big change from his previous way of living. Alma put his sights on Brigham Young University (BYU), where he started studying to become more than just an athlete, leaving behind the fields of Parowan and the security of his family. Alma immersed himself in academic courses at BYU, learning how to think critically, evaluate, and reason in ways that would benefit him in both his personal and athletic lives, in addition to solving equations.

However, stopping there wasn't sufficient. Alma understood that he needed to go outside BYU's boundaries to genuinely broaden his knowledge and create opportunities for the kind of future he had in mind for himself. His focus shifted to Cornell University, one of the most prestigious universities in the US, where he would have the chance to further broaden his horizons in addition to continuing his education. He was called to Cornell not only to seek a legal degree but also to immerse himself in a culture that not only supported but also demanded intellectual endeavors.

For Alma, attending Cornell University was the next step up. His inherent curiosity might be cultivated and honed there, and his need for information could be satisfied. Alma journeyed to Ithaca, New York, a world away from the arid deserts and undulating hills of Utah, leaving behind the comfortable surroundings of the Western

United States. Even though the academic and athletic worlds were very different, Alma's strategy stayed the same: she was focused, hardworking, and driven to win.

Alma's intellectual horizons widened at Cornell in ways he never could have predicted. He pursued a career in law, which enabled him to use his analytical abilities, and discovered that he was exceptionally good in areas that had previously appeared unimportant. The notion he might influence things outside of the physical world through education and that his mind could grow to be as strong as his body had been during his athletic career, however, was more intriguing to him than the legal books alone.

Alma believed that education was about more than just learning; it was about influencing his history and influencing his future. Discipline, hard effort, and a dedication to greatness were the guiding principles that had led him from his days working the farm, and they continued during his time at Cornell, which represented a dramatic shift in his trajectory. Alma now focused on his academic work with the same intensity that he had used to train his body for the high jump.

The Call to Teach and Cornell: A Shift in Focus

More than just a stride in the quest for knowledge, Alma Richards' choice to enroll at Cornell University to seek a law degree marked a sea change in his life. It was the time when his cerebral power, which he was cultivating in the classroom, started to blend with the unadulterated skill he had shown in the physical arena. But as Alma progressed through his coursework and refined his legal knowledge, he started to see a new course emerge—one that would eventually take him into teaching.

Alma had always dreamed of being a teacher, even before he attended Cornell. Alma had always been passionate about helping others, even though his Olympic success had made him more well-known. He was driven to apply his knowledge to improve the lives of others with the same tenacity that had enabled him to excel in sports. Not only did he want to succeed for his reason, but he also wanted to coach others with similar goals and objectives and share what he had learned.

For Alma, teaching was a logical next step. His time at Cornell had cemented his conviction that education was about more than just gaining knowledge for one's benefit; it was also about imparting that knowledge, fostering the development of others, and creating a legacy that might endure a lifetime. Alma already knew that hard effort and determination were the keys to greatness, but he could teach others these principles only via education. His perspective changed from one of rivalry to one of enabling others to compete for themselves.

Alma returned to the West after finishing his education and accepted a teaching position at Venice High School in Los Angeles. The significant change that had occurred within him during his time at Cornell was reflected in his new employment. Alma was no longer just an athlete; he had developed into a wise and kind guy who saw the importance of education and was now able to give back.

Immediately he established a reputation as a considerate and committed educator at Venice High School. He applied the same concentration and discipline that had served him well during his sporting career to his teaching. Alma's students realized that he was teaching them more than simply the basics of science; he was teaching them how to live a purposeful and committed life. Alma's influence on his pupils extended outside of the classroom. He encouraged them to strive for their own goals and aspirations, just as he had done.

During this period, Alma came to fully appreciate the power of education—not as a means to a goal, but as a tool for bringing about change and enabling people to realize their greatest potential. Alma was assisting others in leaping toward their own accomplishments, much like he had jumped higher than anyone had anticipated in the high jump. He was influencing futures as much as minds.

Alma discovered that his teaching style was based on the lessons he had gained as an athlete as his career as an instructor took off. He instilled in his students the same work ethic, perseverance, and conviction in one's abilities that had earned him Olympic gold. Alma had learned that genuine greatness was more about the legacy you left behind and the influence you had on other people than it was about the recognition you received. Alma was also creating a legacy in the classroom that will last much longer than any gold medal.

Alma Richards' move from the sports industry to academics was more than just a professional change; it was a shift in focus from personal achievement to group empowerment. From the young ranch hand with a natural knack for high leaping to the reflective teacher who used his experiences to mold the minds of future generations, it was evidence of his development as a person. From the dusty fields of Parowan to the classrooms of Venice High School, where he taught others the lessons of his own life, Alma's journey had come full circle.

Chapter eight

Shaping Young Minds

Teaching Life: Alma Richards the Instructor

Alma Richards' transition from Olympic gold medalist to schoolteacher was a shift in purpose more than just a career change. His life could have gone in a lot of different directions following his spectacular victory at the Stockholm Olympics in 1912. He took the option to take advantage of the benefits that came with being a well-known athlete and concentrate just on his notoriety. Alma, however, had a more profound idea. He aimed to leave a lasting impression rather than just take home gold. That ambition brought him to the classroom, where he would go on to impact innumerable lives through the values he instilled in his students as well as the knowledge he taught.

Being a teacher was a logical progression of Alma's personality. Alma knew the need for discipline because he had grown up working in the Parowan fields, where every action was the direct result of dedication and hard work. It was about more than simply knowledge; it was about applying that knowledge, about tenacity, and about striving for success both inside and outside of the classroom. He was aware that the lessons he had gained from athletics—the value of perseverance, practice, and focus—applied to his studies just as much as they did on the track.

Alma was able to impart those ideas to a new generation of students when he chose to teach at Venice High School in Los Angeles. In addition to studying science and law, his students were also learning about life, how to overcome obstacles, and how to approach problems. Alma had a distinct viewpoint because of his experience as an Olympic winner. He was more than just a teacher with subject-matter expertise; he was a person who had conquered obstacles. And because of this experience, he was able to mentor his students in ways that textbooks couldn't.

Alma served as a mentor, advisor, and inspiration in the classroom in addition to being a symbol of authority. His work ethic and perseverance, which propelled him to achieve success in his sports career, were mirrored in his teaching manner. Alma wanted his children to learn more than simply knowledge; he wanted them to know the importance of working hard, establishing objectives, and persevering through difficult times. In addition to being a teacher, his students recognized him as a living embodiment of the values he instilled in them.

His personal experiences served as the foundation for his instructional style. Alma was aware that failure was frequently a necessary part of the trip and that the path to accomplishment was rarely clear-cut. Failure was not something to be dreaded in his classroom; rather, it was an opportunity to grow. He taught his students that they could conquer any challenge if they worked hard and persevered, and that their failures were chances to improve.

However, Alma was teaching more than just resiliency; he was emphasizing the importance of education in general. After years of perseverance and hard work, Alma finally made it to Cornell University, where she realized the transformational power of education. For him, education was a method to broaden one's perspectives and overcome the constraints that society frequently placed on people, not merely a ticket to a job or a title. Alma's own experience served as evidence that anyone could succeed if they were prepared to work hard, regardless of background.

Alma taught his students how to think critically, how to examine the world around them, and how to tackle obstacles with an open mind as he helped them on their educational journeys. He did not only teach them how to memorize facts or pass tests. In addition to his achievements, his students held him in high regard for the manner he lived. They observed that he was not only able to excel in one area but had done so in several. From his athletic career to his studies at Cornell, Alma showed that striving for perfection wasn't restricted to a single aspect of life. It was an ongoing undertaking that permeated every part of his life.

Education in Alma's classroom went beyond what was found in a textbook. Most importantly, his students were inspired, uplifted, and supported. They saw in him more than simply a teacher; they saw a man who had lived a life characterized by diligence, fortitude, and an unquenchable curiosity. Alma had an impact that extended beyond the classroom. He gave his students the conviction that education was the key to releasing their potential, that they, too, could overcome hardship, and that they, too, could pursue achievement.

Teachings Outside of the Textbook: Motivating a New Generation

Alma Richards' influence as a teacher went well beyond the legal or scientific teachings he taught his pupils. The way he encouraged them to reflect, to ask questions, and to develop as people was his real legacy. Alma's instruction went beyond the rigid framework of the curriculum, influencing his students' lives in ways that gave them a feeling of direction and resolve as they faced the outside world.

Alma's ability to relate to pupils was what made him unique. He regarded them as potential persons with their distinct skills and challenges, rather than merely as students who needed to finish assignments or pass tests. In all that Alma did, his empathy for his students was clear. Instead of merely lecturing from the front of the room, he interacted with his students, heard their worries, and provided support when required. He used a holistic approach, understanding that education encompassed both academic and personal development.

The importance of diligence and tenacity was among Alma's most significant teachings. Success, his kids realized, was about coming up every day, putting in the work, and getting better, not about having innate talent or being the greatest right away. Alma frequently illustrated this notion with examples from his athletic career. He would explain to his students that he had no official high-jumping training when he was younger. Nevertheless, he had advanced to the top levels of competition via unrelenting practice and commitment. Alma's narrative served as a potent reminder that anything worthwhile took dedication, perseverance, and hard work.

However, Alma taught more than simply work ethic. Additionally, he instilled in his students the value of critical thinking and questioning the established quo. Because of his academic training, he firmly believed that education could change the world. Alma urged his pupils to never be content with flimsy responses, to always ask questions, and to look for fresh viewpoints. He recognized the complexity of the world and the importance of education in comprehending it. His pupils gained the ability to think critically, come up with solutions based on more than just memory, and approach challenges with an open mind.

Alma's teachings on leadership, honesty, and character were equally as impactful as her intellectual understanding. He set an example for his students, demonstrating to them that genuine leadership was about helping others, taking responsibility, and doing the right thing even when it was challenging, not about fame or fortune. Alma's life had been a living example of these principles. Although his Olympic gold medal was amazing, what made him stand out was his dedication to his community, family, and education. He demonstrated to his students that helping others was just as important to success in life as what one achieved for oneself.

Alma had a significant impact that extended way beyond his generation. Numerous of his pupils went on to become independent leaders, including doctors, attorneys, educators, and activists, and they gave Alma credit for motivating them to realize their greatest potential. His influence extended beyond his time in the classroom, influencing the lives of innumerable others who subsequently made significant contributions to society.

In addition to the knowledge he taught, his teaching legacy also includes the lives he impacted, the minds he molded, and the values he instilled in the following generation. Alma's impact extended beyond the classroom and into his students' hearts and minds, motivating them to study hard, think critically, and lead moral lives.

Chapter nine

The Genesis of the Film

Discovering the Past: The Rediscovered Story of Alma Richards

Like many great historical personalities, Alma Richards had a life full of accomplishments, but for a while, it seemed to be all but forgotten. His victory in the high jump at the 1912 Stockholm Olympics, where he won the gold medal, was a significant milestone in American sports history. However, Alma's story vanished from the public consciousness after her moment of fame. Alma's life changed in the years after his sporting achievements; he became a teacher, a mentor, and a quiet leader in his community. Nevertheless, the renown that had enveloped him started to fade.

Only as time went on would Alma Richards' tale be rediscovered—and not by chance, but thanks to the efforts of a few tenacious people who felt that his life, his trip, and his accomplishments were too significant to be lost to the records of the past. Alma Richards' tale was rediscovered as a result of the combined efforts of historians, filmmakers, and sports fans who saw a gap in the literature about Olympic heroes of the early 20th century. Even though Alma's name was once inscribed in history books, other athletes and historical occurrences have eclipsed it.

The serious investigation into Alma's background started when T.C. While studying the history of Olympic competitors, Christensen, a director who has a strong interest in historical sports figures, found Alma's name. T.C. had always been captivated by tales of athletes who, despite their modest upbringing, achieved greatness with tenacity and willpower. After hearing that Alma Richards had won a gold medal, T.C. acknowledged the enormous potential for a movie that would not only honor Alma's accomplishments but also provide insight into his extraordinary journey, which was based on perseverance, faith in oneself, and the ability of sports to change people's lives.

Finding out about Alma's life was the first challenge. In the decades that followed his Olympic triumph, not much had been published about him. In contrast to other sportsmen who had achieved widespread fame, Alma's narrative had not received much attention in the history of athletics. This presented T.C. with a major obstacle. and his group, but they remained unfazed. They interviewed Alma's surviving family members, searched through old newspapers, and delved into local archives; all of them were profoundly appreciative of the influence he had left behind. Alma's story gradually came to light, not only as a remarkable sporting achievement but also as one of fortitude, modesty, and the quiet strength of a man who had accomplished greatness in many ways.

The entirety of Alma's life, his journey from athlete to educator, and the way he used his position to motivate future generations comprised his legacy, which went beyond just his gold medal. His life was characterized by his capacity to rise above the circumstances he was born into, to transcend the constraints society placed on him, and to impart the lessons he had learned to others—not only by the physical act of jumping over a bar. These were the attributes that T.C. and his group believed they had to be filmed.

It became evident that Alma's story was more than just an athletic biography as the historical pieces began to come together. It was a tale of human tenacity that spoke to everyone who had ever suffered or tried to accomplish something against all odds, regardless of whether they were involved in sports or not. Alma's life exemplified a common theme: the value of self-belief against external pressures, the strength of willpower, and the victory of the human spirit.

From Concept to Screenplay: Developing the Story for the Large Screen

Following Alma's story's rediscovery, the next obstacle was turning it into a script, which called for considerable thought and a profound regard for the subject. The story of Alma Richards was everything from simple. It was the story of a youngster from Parowan, Utah, who had overcome societal and personal constraints, fought the odds, and accomplished something remarkable—not merely the story of a man who won a gold medal. It was necessary to write this story in a way that would both accurately depict historical events and convey the spirit of Alma's journey.

T.C. Christensen spent months creating the story of Alma's life with his writing team. The screenplay was created to examine the underlying themes of sacrifice, family, and personal development in addition to showcasing his athletic accomplishments. The movie needed to show

Alma's inner conflict and his aspiration to become great despite his circumstances. Naturally, the plot revolves around the high jump competition, but it is more than just a physical contest; it serves as a metaphor for Alma's whole existence. Every jump stood for a challenge he had to face as a person and as an athlete.

The filmmakers had to strike a careful balance in telling the story. Although Alma's narrative was one of personal success, it also captured the hardships of a whole generation. At the time of his Olympic victory in 1912, many Americans were still dealing with the fallout from the early 20th century, which was characterized by social unrest, economic hardship, and the rise of new industries that frequently left those living in smaller, rural communities behind. Alma's achievement was not only a personal triumph; it was also a triumph for the working class, who, like him, were attempting to make their mark in a society that frequently appeared to favor the powerful and wealthy.

The emotional impact of Alma's transformation from athlete to teacher also needed to be conveyed in the writing. After leaving the world of sports, he spent a crucial period of his life working as an instructor. Alma saw it as an opportunity to return the favor to the world that had given him so much, not just a change in his work. He wanted to impart to the next generation the lessons he had learned about the importance of hard work and knowledge. He had a silent impact throughout his tenure as a teacher at Venice High School in Los Angeles. Alma taught life lessons in addition to science.

As the screenplay developed, it became evident that Alma's tale would appeal to viewers outside of the sports industry. His life served as an example of the universal battle to persevere in the face of adversity, to stand up for what one believes in, and to overcome personal hurdles. These topics needed to be presented in a way that was uplifting, accessible, and real.

The filmmakers had to think about Alma's life's visual portrayal in addition to the story. It was no easy task to film the high jump itself. To convey the elegance and beauty of Alma's technique, the high jump required a dynamic and accurate portrayal. The filmmakers put a lot of effort into recreating the Olympic scene in a way that would honor Alma's triumph since every leap had to feel as genuine as the emotion that accompanied it. The Olympic stadium scenes were shot with a focus on historical authenticity, paying close attention to the atmosphere and appearance of the period. The filmmakers aimed to create a visual universe that took viewers back to 1912, when Alma Richards created history, down to the stadium's outfits.

The directors focused on casting Alma Richards in the lead role after finishing the screenplay and putting the visual components in place. In addition to portraying Alma's physical attributes, the actor had to capture the quiet fortitude and tenacity that had characterized his existence. Following a thorough search, a gifted actress was selected to play Alma's story; this choice would be crucial in guaranteeing that the character's emotional range was accurately captured on screen.

Converting Alma Richards' narrative into a movie was a labor of love that involved teamwork, investigation, and a common desire to communicate a long-overdue tale. Profoundly impacted by Alma's journey, the filmmakers aimed to respect his legacy while producing a movie that would motivate contemporary viewers. It was an important story to tell, not just for the benefit of history but also for the benefit of future generations who may be motivated by Alma's steadfast dedication to his objectives, his fortitude in the face of difficulty, and his significant influence as a mentor and teacher.

Raising the Bar: The Alma Richards Story will be released in the United States on April 30, 2025, and it is currently available in a few international locations. For those who haven't seen it yet, the movie is more than just a recounting of an Olympic triumph; it's a celebration of a life well lived, an ode to the strength of willpower, and a reminder that greatness stems not from wealth or fame but rather from the drive to aim higher. In addition to inspiring generations throughout his life, Alma Richards' narrative will now inspire generations to come thanks to film.

Chapter ten

Lights, Camera, Action

Bringing the Characters to Life: Casting the Vision

It was no easy task to turn Alma Richards' extraordinary life into a motion picture. Capturing Alma's attitude and the life-changing experience that took him from a poor farm lad in Parowan, Utah, to an Olympic gold champion was more important than simply documenting the facts. In addition to excellent writing and directing, a cast that could capture the essence of this remarkable man and the others who influenced his tale was necessary to bring such a multifaceted and nuanced person to life on screen.

Finding the appropriate performers for the important parts was a top priority for the filmmakers when they cast Raising the Bar: The Alma Richards Story. Alma's life was an emotional journey characterized by internal conflicts, self-discovery, and victory rather than merely a sequence of occurrences. Alma Richards had to be

79

presented as a guy of great integrity, humility, and fortitude in addition to being a gifted athlete. A performer who could embody Alma's calm resolve and inner fortitude was what the directors were looking for.

They searched far and wide before settling on a gifted actor who possessed the ideal balance of emotional nuance and physicality. In addition to being able to replicate the athleticism of a high jumper, the actor selected to play Alma Richards was able to provide a complex, vulnerable portrayal of a man battling self-doubt, personal development, and the pressure to live up to others' expectations. It was difficult to cast Alma since it called for a unique blend of athletic prowess and in-depth knowledge of the character's emotional journey.

However, Alma was not the only choice in the casting. The depth of the supporting cast, who played a pivotal role in influencing Alma's life and growth, was essential to the movie's success. The same attention to detail and genuineness have to be given to the portrayal of Alma's coach, family, and other significant figures in his trip. The directors were looking for actors who could embody the love, sacrifice, and support that characterized Alma's parents' relationship with Alma. They served as the dependable cornerstones of his early years, and their image needed to convey the constant assistance they gave him along the way.

Another important aspect of the movie was the portrayal of Professor Hensley, the mentor who initially ignited Alma's passion for learning and sports. The direction and support that inspired Alma to follow his aspirations had to be reflected in this persona. To inspire the audience as much as it inspired Alma in the novel, the actor selected for this part needed to exude knowledge, kindness, and faith in Alma's abilities.

The goal of casting these characters was to create a dynamic that would appeal to the viewers rather than merely filling parts. In addition to embodying the historical figure they were playing, each actor had to contribute their comprehension of the emotional significance of the events. To guarantee that the performances were based on authenticity and that each exchange, glance, and sentence felt like a genuine representation of Alma's life, the casting crew collaborated closely with the director.

However, the primary characters weren't the only focus of the casting process. The 1912 Stockholm Olympics served as the setting for the movie, and the ambiance of the occasion needed to be meticulously recreated. The athletes, extras, and onlookers in the backdrop needed to feel as though they were a part of Alma's universe. From the athletes' attire to the subtle body language of those surrounding Alma throughout the Games, the filmmakers collaborated with a group of historians and costume designers to make sure that every element was historically authentic.

The producers knew they had put together a collection of gifted people who could bring the emotional depth of Alma's narrative to life as soon as the cast was set. However, casting was just one aspect of the situation. Filming the journey that would take viewers from Alma's modest origins to the Olympic podium was the true labor that remained.

Recording the Trip: Reenacting Emotion and History

It took more than just reenacting historical events to bring Alma Richards' story to life on screen; it also required conveying the emotional core of his trip. The producers were aware that the film's success depended on their capacity to capture not only Alma's life events but also the emotions that motivated him to achieve greatness. The subtleties were crucial to making every leap, every moment of uncertainty, and every victory felt genuine.

The construction of the set pieces marked the start of the filming phase. It was no easy task to recreate the Olympic Stadium in 1912. The goal of the film was to give viewers the impression that they were inside the stadium where Alma made his Olympic debut. From the grandstands to the track and field area, the crew painstakingly reconstructed the stadium's appearance with the assistance of historians and set designers. In addition to being historically accurate, the movie's images were created to recreate the majesty and intensity of the Olympic Games in a way that put viewers right there with the action.

However, the goal was to capture the spirit of Alma's emotional journey, not just the physical surroundings. The hardships and tenacity that molded Alma's ascent to fame had to be portrayed in the movie. To achieve this, the actors and the director collaborated closely to produce emotionally charged scenes. The timing of the movie was designed to create tension while gradually exposing

Alma's inner conflicts, his periods of uncertainty, and his eventual epiphany.

Alma's actual Olympic high leap was one of the most impactful scenes to capture on camera. The filmmakers were aware that this scene needed to serve as the film's emotional focal point. It was more than just a sporting event; it was the result of Alma's labors. The filmmakers used a combination of real-world stunts, computer-generated imagery, and meticulous editing to make the jump seem realistic. In addition to being a metaphor for the emotional leaps Alma had made throughout his life, the jump had to be a tangible embodiment of his spirit—his undeveloped, unadulterated potential.

To highlight Alma's grace and athleticism, the action was shot from a variety of perspectives. The audience was able to appreciate both the jump's physicality and emotional impact because the producers employed slow motion to portray the smoothness of his motions. Alma's jump over the bar served as a metaphor for the challenges he had surmounted throughout his life, both real and imagined. In every way, it was the time he showed the world that even the most modest upbringing could lead to greatness.

Emotional depth was just as important as technical accuracy while filming the high jump scenario. To make the jump seem like the pinnacle of Alma's quest, the director and actors put in many hours of work. He needed those few seconds when he flew over the bar to represent every ounce of effort that had gone into his training, his faith in himself, and his perseverance. As Alma landed, his expression expressing his amazement at what he had just done, it was more than just a sporting triumph; it was the moment that would make him a champion of all time.

However, the movie was about more than just the high jump. The producers also intended to examine Alma's more private and subdued moments. His path to the Olympics involved much more than just sports, from his early farm days to his time at Cornell and Brigham Young University. It was about the relationships that molded Alma, about his desire to go against the grain, and about self-discovery. The film maintained the emotional undercurrent of Alma's life throughout by capturing these times with the same care and attention to detail as the Olympic scenes.

As a result, the movie explored more than just athletic success; it also explored the strength of character, the power of tenacity, and the unwavering conviction that anything is achievable with enough effort. Raising the Bar: The Alma Richards Story evolved into a celebration of the human spirit and what is possible when one never gives up on their aspirations, rather than merely being a sports film.

The actors and crew realized they had something unique as the last sequences were being shot. In addition to telling Alma Richards' story to a new generation, the movie would serve as a reminder to viewers worldwide of the strength of willpower, the worth of perseverance, and the significance of having faith in oneself despite all obstacles.

Chapter eleven

Echoes of a Remarkable Life

Alma Richards: His Significance in the History of Sport

Not only was Alma Richards' triumph at the 1912 Stockholm Olympics a personal accomplishment, but it also signaled a turning point in American sports history. Even while the high jump competition is legendary in and of itself, it gave Richards the chance to make his mark on sports history. Although Alma Richards' narrative has not been portrayed as frequently as that of some of his Olympic peers, there is no denying his impact on both the sport and those around him. Because of its simplicity and significant impact, his life continues to inspire and resonate not only in the sports community but also outside of it, serving as a testament to what can be accomplished in the face of adversity.

Alma holds a special place in sports history, especially in the US, for a number of reasons. The Olympics were still in their infancy when he won, and many of the participants, like Alma, had backgrounds that were very different from those of professional sports organizations and upscale training facilities. Alma's success served as a much-needed beacon for those who followed him, and his ascent to fame was evidence of his strength of tenacity.

Richards' accomplishment was noteworthy due to the special circumstances that brought him to that point as well as his athletic prowess. He was not raised with the same level of preparation as many contemporary Olympic athletes. Alma was raised in a modest household and her early years were characterized by toil on the farm rather than the demanding training schedules that today characterize the lives of professional athletes. His success came from a combination of natural talent, physical prowess, and—perhaps most importantly—a mental fortitude that motivated him to go above and beyond expectations in all facets of his life, not just in the high jump.

In the years after the Stockholm Games, Alma's name came to represent overcoming hardship. His 1912 gold medal win garnered widespread notice, which raised track and field's stature in the US. Alma was a role model for the upcoming generation of athletes, proving that anyone could succeed through perseverance and hard effort, regardless of background. His Olympic achievement proved that tenacity may triumph over seemingly insurmountable challenges, whether they be monetary, social, or physical.

Even if his name hasn't always been at the forefront of the discourse, Alma's place in sports history has stayed stable throughout time. He carried himself with a quiet dignity throughout his life, which is partly responsible for this. Alma was never one to brag about his accomplishments, and following the Olympics in 1912, he went back to living a life that was more about serving his community than it was about celebrity. Alma's influence extended beyond the realm of sports to his work as a teacher, where he shaped and influenced young people's thinking long after his athletic career was over.

Alma Richards's famous leap on that fatal day in Stockholm is not the only thing that people remember about him. The teachings he taught the world—lessons of humility, perseverance, and the quiet strength of a man who thought that anything was achievable if one was prepared to put in the necessary effort—define his legacy. As time passes,

Alma's impact remains felt in the sports industry and beyond, serving as a constant reminder of what is possible when one puts their all into one's ambitions.

The Durable Strength of an Impossible Victory

The human spirit and the strength of tenacity are demonstrated by Alma Richards' trip from the rocky pastures of Parowan, Utah, to the magnificent Olympic platform in Stockholm. He overcame great physical, social, and financial obstacles to accomplish what many believed was unachievable. Alma's quest is more than just a tale of athletic achievement, though, as it reflects the human fight to overcome one's surroundings, overcome social constraints, and follow one's dreams, no matter how impossible they may seem.

Alma's gold medal win and the circumstances surrounding it are what give his victory such lasting significance. The world was radically different in 1912. The early 20th century was a period of profound social, economic, and cultural transformation in the United States. Athletes frequently lacked the training, facilities, and resources that contemporary competitors have access to because sports were not yet the multibillion-dollar corporations that they are today. To achieve this, Alma, like many of his peers, had to rely on his innate skills, his perseverance, and his unshakable faith in himself.

His triumph in Stockholm, a city distant from Utah's dry plains, represented something far more significant than mere sporting success. For everyone who had ever been told that their history, station in life, or lack of resources prevented them from succeeding, it was a victory. Because Alma's narrative was about regular people accomplishing great things, it struck a chord with individuals from all walks of life. Alma's improbable victory demonstrated to the world that anyone who was prepared to put in the necessary effort on their trade, regardless of their circumstances, could succeed.

The message that Alma Richards' win conveys is what gives it its lasting impact. It is a message of optimism, fortitude, and the conviction that, with the correct mix of hard work, tenacity, and faith in oneself, one can always overcome obstacles. For everyone who has ever encountered challenges in their life, Alma's win was a moment of collective triumph rather than only a personal accomplishment. For others who had been disregarded, undervalued, or ostracized, his gold medal served as a ray of hope. It gave them hope that they, too, could overcome their situation and become great.

Alma's impact kept expanding even after he retired from competitive sports and went back to teaching. His deeds, his devotion to his kids, and his ongoing commitment to his community screamed louder than any medal could, so he didn't need the limelight to have an impact. Alma realized that genuine greatness was about making a difference in other people's lives, not about receiving awards. And in that sense, no gold medal could ever fully capture his legacy as a teacher, mentor, and community leader.

Even now, the effects of Alma Richards' extraordinary life are still felt. His narrative is still among the most impactful in American sports history, even though his name may not constantly be in the news or mentioned in the same context as other Olympic greats. Every athlete who has ever battled to overcome adversity, every student who has ever been inspired to pursue their goals, and every individual who has ever trusted in the strength of perseverance and self-belief are all influenced by Alma.

Alma Richards' victory was a leap into history rather than merely a jump over a bar. His tale did not finish with his Olympic win in 1912; rather, it marked the start of a legacy that has inspired generations of people. His path serves as a reminder that greatness is determined by where we are willing to go and how hard we are willing to work to get there, not by where we start. Alma's victory ultimately served as a reminder to all of us that, with enough willpower and passion, we too can achieve greater things than we ever imagined.

Alma Richards' victory was a leap into history rather than merely a jump over a bar. His tale did not finish with his Olympic win in 1912; rather it marked the start of a legacy that has inspired generations of people. His path serves as a reminder that greatness is determined by where we are willing to go and how hard we are willing to work to get there, not by where we start. Alma's victory ultimately served as a reminder to all of us that, with enough willpower and passion, we too can achieve greater things than we ever imagined.

Made in the USA
Monee, IL
17 August 2025

Made in the USA
Monee, IL
17 August 2025